The Pearl

John Steinbeck

STUDENT PACKET

NOTE:

The trade book edition of the novel used to prepare this guide is found in the Novel Units catalog and on the Novel Units website. Using other editions may have varied page references.

Please note: We have assigned Interest Levels based on our knowledge of the themes and ideas of the books included in the Novel Units sets, however, please assess the appropriateness of this novel or trade book for the age level and maturity of your students prior to reading with them. You know your students best!

ISBN 978-1-56137-326-0

Copyright infringement is a violation of Federal Law.

© 2020 by Novel Units, Inc., St. Louis, MO. All rights reserved. No part of this publication may be reproduced, translated, stored in a retrieval system, or transmitted in any way or by any means (electronic, mechanical, photocopying, recording, or otherwise) without prior written permission from Novel Units, Inc.

Reproduction of any part of this publication for an entire school or for a school system, by for-profit institutions and tutoring centers, or for commercial sale is strictly prohibited.

Novel Units is a registered trademark of Conn Education.

Printed in the United States of America.

To order, contact your
local school supply store, or:

Toll-Free Fax: 877.716.7272
Phone: 888.650.4224
3901 Union Blvd., Suite 155
St. Louis, MO 63115

sales@novelunits.com

novelunits.com

Name_____

The Pearl
Student Worksheet #1
Vocabulary—Chapter 1

Sometimes words you are looking for do not appear in a standard dictionary. You will probably need to consult an unabridged dictionary for the definitions of these words.

1. pulque _____

2. bougainvillaea _____

3. In what kind of book could you see pictures of the plants related to these words?
   _____

Sometimes words are defined with other words with which you are unfamiliar. Look up and write definitions for:

4. lymphatic _____

5. scorpion _____

6. What kind of book would tell you more about the lymph system?
   _____

7. Where could you find a picture of a scorpion?
   _____

If you know one word, sometimes it helps you remember another. Explain how the words paired below are related in meaning.

8. supple • suppliant

9. substitute • subsequent

10. coven • covey

You can often guess the meanings of words on standardized matching tests if you know the parts of speech. Try these:

11. _____ parable (n.)
12. _____ plaintively (adv.)
13. _____ feinted (v.)
14. _____ indigent (adj.)

a. mournfully
b. story with a moral lesson
c. poor
d. pretended

© Novel Units, Inc.   All rights reserved

Name_____

The Pearl
Student Worksheet #2
Vocabulary—Chapters 2 and 3

Three of the words in each line are synonyms. Circle the word that is not a synonym.

1. estuary   river mouth   crest   delta
2. oscillate   wave   undulate   defray
3. palisade   bulwark   bullock   wall
4. hillock   hammock   hill   hummock
5. treatment   remedy   stimulant   poultice
6. contemplative   reflective   validated   speculative
7. mirage   oasis   illusion   hallucination
8. lustrous   luminous   subdued   incandescent

Find each word in the right-hand column in the text. Page numbers are provided. Reread the sentence in which the word appears. Then use context clues to match the definitions on the left with the words. Check your answers with a dictionary.

____ 9. judicious (28)
____ 10. disparagement (32)
____ 11. subjugation (38)
____ 12. semblance (29)
____ 13. prophecy (33)
____ 14. dissembling (42)
____ 15. precipitated (30)
____ 16. transfigured (34)
____ 17. furtive (48)
____ 18. lucent (32)
____ 19. benediction (35)
____ 20. cozened (51)

a. totally changed
b. disrespect, belittlement
c. shining richly
d. disguising
e. cheated
f. make subservient by force
g. invocation of favor or blessing
h. appearance
i. showing good judgement
j. caused or hurried an event
k. stealthy; sneaky
l. vision of the future

© Novel Units, Inc.   All rights reserved

Name_____

The Pearl
Student Worksheet #3
Vocabulary—Chapters 4 and 5

countenanced (54)	stalwart (60)	legerdemain (62)
spurned (64)	lethargy (71)	skirled (80)
exhilaration (81)	keening (83)	leprosy (84)

The class should divide into nine small groups. Each group is responsible for mapping one word on the list on the word map below. Each group must also create a charade representing the word, and present it to the class before sharing their word map.

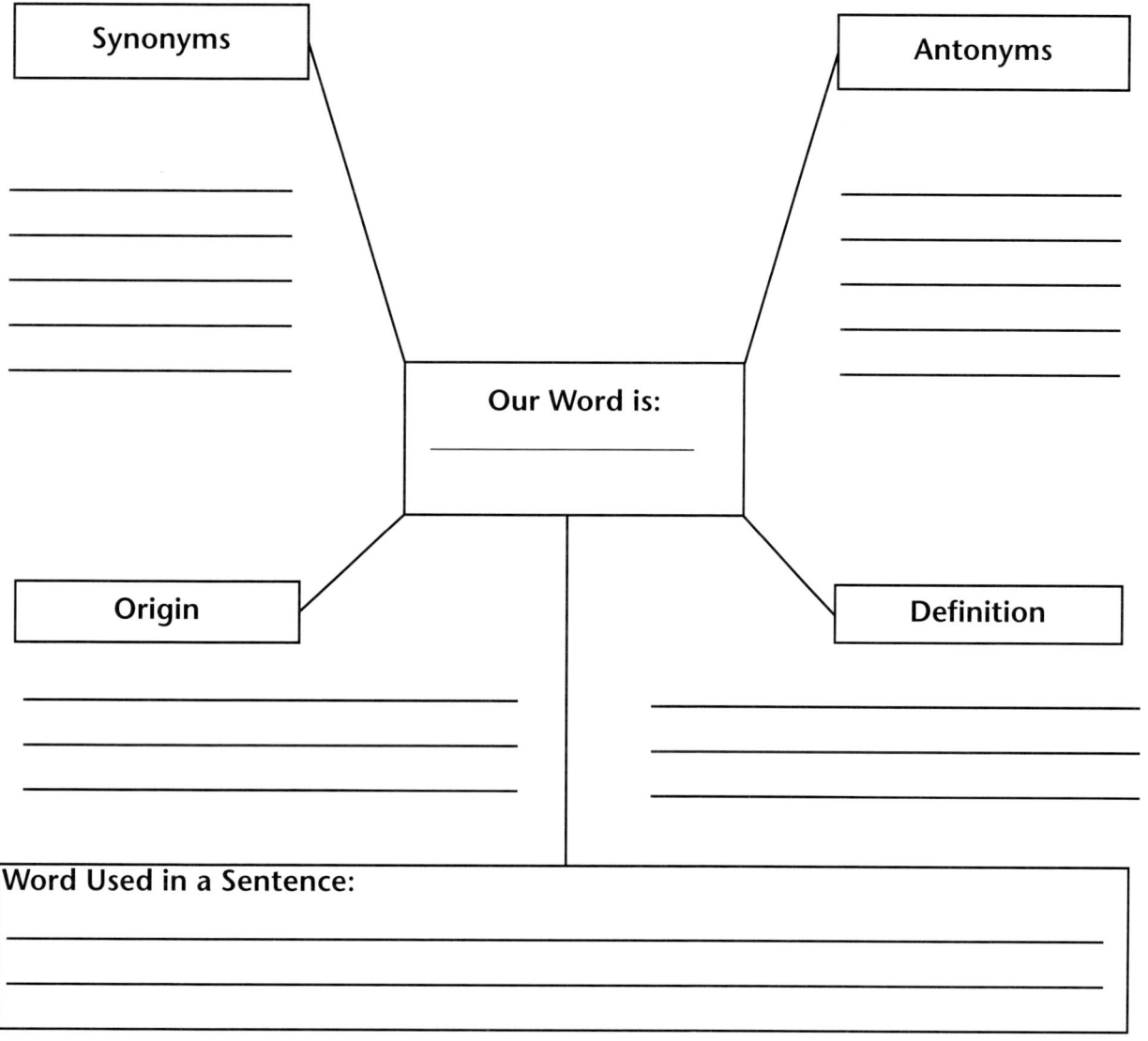

© Novel Units, Inc.   All rights reserved

Name_____

The Pearl
Student Worksheet #4
Vocabulary—Chapter 6

Use a thesaurus to complete the synonym trains below. You may need to use the dictionary first to find a simpler word and then look that word up in the thesaurus.

sinister			
guttural			
monolithic			
irresolution			
escarpment			
petulant			
intercession			
germane			

Name_____

The Pearl
Study Guide

Chapter One

1. Who are the three important characters?

2. Describe each character.
   a.

   b.

   c.

3. What kind of lifestyle do they have?

4. What evidence of belief in superstition can you find?

5. Copy several examples from the novel that show the author's use of description.
   a.

   b.

   c.

6. With what event in this chapter does the real action of the story begin?

7. Show how Kino's life is symbolized in "songs." What contrasting songs are emphasized at different times? What is the purpose of including the songs?

Name_____

The Pearl
Study Guide • 2

8. What is the difference between the "city of grass huts" and the "city of stone"? How are we made aware of the difference?

9. In Chapter One, we meet the doctor. Three different characterizations of the doctor are suggested. Distinguish between them:
   a. the doctor as seen by the beggars

   b. the doctor as seen by himself

   c. the doctor as seen by Kino

Chapter Two

10. Use at least three details about the town to make inferences about the lifestyle of the villagers.
    a.

    b.

    c.

11. What object of great value had Kino's grandfather brought from Nayarit, and why was it so valuable?

12. How are pearls created by oysters?

13. Describe how Kino searched for pearls.

14. Why do Kino's people sing songs? Give an example of a song, and tell why it was sung.

Name_____

The Pearl
Study Guide • 3

15. Why does Kino want to save one particular oyster to open last?

16. After Kino finds the great pearl, what happens to Coyotito?

Chapter Three

17. Kino and Juana thought everyone shared their joy—but what was really happening?

18. To what evils does Steinbeck compare the evil growing in the town?

19. What was so important about Coyotito going to school?

20. How did the doctor trick Kino and Juana?

21. What happened in the middle of the night?

Chapter Four

22. In selling the pearl, what disadvantages and advantages did Kino have?
    a. disadvantages

    b. advantages

23. Can you explain the attitude the dealers had toward Kino and his "Pearl of the World"?

24. How did the townspeople react to what happened?

25. By the end of Chapter 4, what decision had Kino reached? What helped him to make this decision? Was he right or wrong?

© Novel Units, Inc.   All rights reserved

Name_____

The Pearl
Study Guide • 4

Chapter Five

26. With what important incident did this chapter begin? Can you explain Juana's actions?

27. What incident in this chapter put peace behind Kino and Juana forever?

28. What additional events made it impossible for Kino and Juana to remain in the village?

29. How did Kino and Juana spend their last day in the village?

30. By the end of this chapter, the pearl has become a moral issue to Kino. How does he express it? How do you explain it?

Chapter Six

31. How does the author describe Kino at the beginning of this chapter?

32. This chapter might be subtitled "the flight." Trace it through the important incidents that happened.

33. Describe the return of the family to the village.

34. Can you explain Kino's final action?

35. Now that you have finished reading the book, can you explain why the foreword says this story might be a parable?

Name_____

The Pearl
Vocabulary Quiz
Use After Reading

In the blank, put the letter of the word that best fits the sentence.

```
a. indigent          f. bulwark          k. transfigured
b. suppliant         g. precipitated     l. petulant
c. estuary           h. incandescence    m. germane
d. poultice          i. lethargy         n. monolithic
e. speculatively     j. undulating       o. semblance
```

1. "The town lay on a broad _____, its old yellow plastered buildings hugging the beach."

2. "A canoe is a _____ against starvation."

3. "It (the pearl) captured the light and refined it and gave it back in silver _____."

4. "The essence of pearl mixed with the essence of men, and a curious dark residue was _____."

5. "A _____ had settled on him, and a little gray hopelessness."

6. "The baby was weary and _____, and he cried softly."

7. "Any sound that was not _____ to the night would make them alert."

8. "He looked _____ at the basket."

9. "She gathered some brown seaweed and made a flat damp _____ of it…"

10. "But ahead were the naked granite mountains, rising out of erosion rubble and standing _____ against the sky."

11. The doctor refused to treat an _____ baby with a scorpion bite.

12. "Slowly he put his _____ hat on his head."

13. "Above, the water was an _____ mirror of brightness."

14. "He kept these agents in separate offices to give a _____ of competition."

15. "He was a man _____."

Name_____

The Pearl
Chapter One Quiz
Use After Reading Chapter One

1. Describe Kino.

2. What is the "Song of the Family"?

3. What was on the rope in the baby's box?

4. How does Juana show that she is superstitious?

5. What group of people know everything about the town?

6. Why does Kino seem to hate and fear the doctor at the same time?

7. Why does the doctor refuse to treat Coyotito?

8. Define "indigene."

9. What place does the doctor dream of?

10. Where does the doctor's servant tell Kino the doctor has gone?

Name_____

The Pearl
Chapters Two and Three Quiz
Use After Reading Chapters Two and Three

1. Define "estuary."

2. Why is Kino's canoe so precious to him?

3. For what does Juana pray directly?

4. In what way is finding the pearl an "accident"?

5. What happened to the baby's scorpion sting as soon as the pearl was found?

6. Name one of Kino's dreams which can be fulfilled because of the pearl.

7. How does the doctor deceive Kino and Juana?

8. Who do you imagine Kino's attackers were? Explain why.

9. How does Kino change after he has formed his plan?

10. Why does Juana want Kino to throw away the pearl?

Name_____

The Pearl
Chapter Four Quiz
Use After Reading Chapter Four

1. What is the name of the town where Kino lives?

2. Who went with Kino and Juana to sell the pearl?

3. How did the pearl buyers operate?

4. Were the buyers usually fair with the villagers?

5. How did the pearl buyers try to trick Kino?

6. What did Kino decide to do with the pearl?

7. Why were some of Kino's neighbors proud of him?

8. Why was Juan Tomás worried for Kino?

9. Kino says that he will not worry because _____ will protect him.

10. At the end of the chapter, what does Juana ask Kino to do with the pearl?

Name_____

The Pearl
Chapter Five Quiz
Use After Reading Chapter Five

1. Why does Juana sneak out of the hut early in the morning?

2. What does Kino do when he catches up with Juana?

3. Why does Juana immediately forgive Kino for his treatment of her?

4. What happened to Kino after he left Juana on the beach?

5. What happened to the pearl?

6. Why did Juana tell Kino that they must flee?

7. What was done to Kino's canoe?

8. What was done to Kino's house?

9. How did Juan Tomás help his brother?

10. What does Juan Tomás tell Kino he should do with the pearl?

Name_____

The Pearl
Chapter Six Quiz
Use After Reading Chapter Six

1. What does Kino begin to act and feel like as he protects his family?

2. What precautions does Kino take to throw his pursuers off the track?

3. Describe Kino's pursuers.

4. Why does Kino want to leave Juana behind?

5. Where do Kino, Juana, and Coyotito hide in the high country?

6. What is Kino's plan to eliminate the pursuers?

7. What went wrong with the plan?

8. Describe Kino and Juana's return to La Paz.

9. What finally happened to the pearl?

10. What do Kino and Juana have left?

Name

The Pearl
Cooperative Project
Student Worksheet #5
Use After Reading

Cooperative Project

Each group is responsible for one of the following topics. Each group should fully discuss, in panel discussion form, the questions posed in its topic. Grades are based on how thoroughly the topics are analyzed in ten to fifteen minutes. Each member of the group is assigned the same grade, so encourage the members in your group to participate fully.

GROUP 1: PLOT
What conflicts lead the story to its climax? Is the plot simple or complex? Do the characters seem to be continuations of who they started out to be, or are they slightly disjointed? (Give examples.) Can you notice rising and falling action in some of the chapters as well as in the book as a whole?

GROUP 2: MAIN CHARACTERS
What is the relationship between Kino and Juana? Between them and their son? How does Steinbeck reveal this family relationship? What do you learn about the characters of Juana and Kino as the novel unfolds? Do their characters change?

GROUP 3: MINOR CHARACTERS
How fully are the minor characters of the novel developed? What importance do the minor characters have in the novel? How are the characters of the doctor, the pearl buyers, and the townspeople as a whole revealed?

GROUP 4: STYLE
What kinds of details are used in the writing style? What do the descriptions of the settings add to the book as a whole? Cite some of these descriptions. The novel has a curious rhythmic quality, almost like that of one of Kino's chants or songs. How is this achieved? Read some good examples of this rhythmic language.

GROUP 5: THEME
Because this novel is a parable and may be seen in many lights, there may be many themes. What are some that your group can suggest? Why did you choose these themes?

GROUP 6: RESOLUTION
Does this novel resolve itself in triumph or defeat? Your group may treat this as a panel discussion or as a debate.

Name_____

The Pearl
Writing Assignment
Student Worksheet #6
Use After Reading

Write Your Own Parable

A parable is a short, simple story from which a lesson or moral may be drawn. The characters in a parable are often representative of other persons, places, or things which pertain to the moral.

Your task is to write a parable. The parable may involve conflicts, ironies, foreshadowing, etc. It may also follow the same developmental form as a short story, from exposition to resolution. The finished parable should be a complete, sensible story that uses your creative energies. The average parable should be 200-300 words in length.

Attach the half-sheet below to your paper and give all the information asked.

Name _____

List the characters in your parable and define the role of each in one sentence.

What is the central symbol in your parable? What does it represent?

In one sentence, state the lesson/moral behind your parable.

Name_____

The Pearl
Student Worksheet #7
Novel Analysis

The Right Decision

In *The Pearl,* as in most novels, the outcome would have been different if certain things had or had not happened. For each "IF" below, write a brief description of how the alternate decision or event would have changed the outcome of the novel.

1. IF Juana had not wanted to take the baby to the doctor, and had been confident that the seaweed poultice would work…

    _____
    _____
    _____
    _____

2. IF one of the pearl buyers had offered a fair price for the pearl out of his own pocket…

    _____
    _____
    _____
    _____

3. IF Kino had thrown the pearl back into the sea the first time Juana suggested it…

    _____
    _____
    _____
    _____

4. IF Kino had given the pearl to the trackers without a struggle…

    _____
    _____
    _____
    _____

Name_____

The Pearl
Student Worksheet #8
Novel Analysis
Use After Reading

The pearl, the central symbol in the novel, symbolizes several different types of evil. Complete the diagram below showing the various kinds of evil that are shown through the characters the pearl affects.

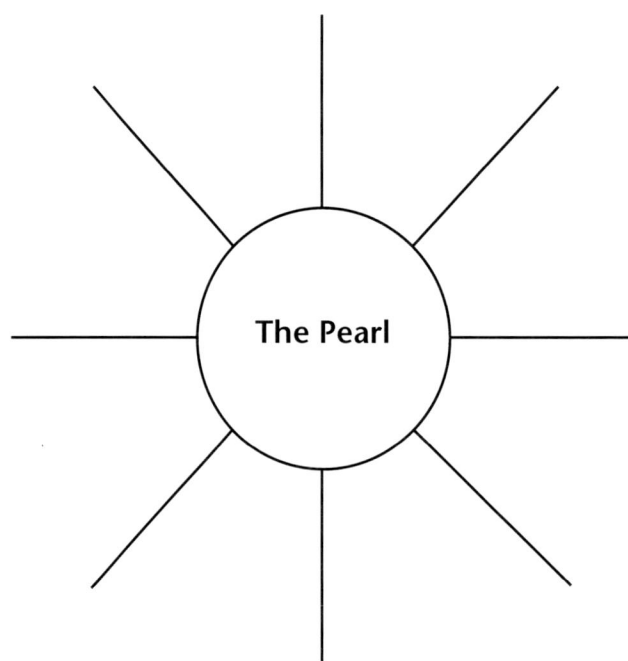

Name_____

The Pearl
Student Worksheet #9
Creative Writing

An education for Coyotito meant everything to Kino because, finally, he would know "what is in the books" and he would be able to see when he was being cheated. In the space below, write a letter to Kino telling him the truth about the priest, the doctor, and the pearl buyers.

Dear Kino,

_____
_____
_____
_____
_____
_____
_____
_____
_____
_____
_____
_____
_____
_____
_____
_____
_____
_____
_____
_____

Sincerely,

_____

Name_____

The Pearl
Student Worksheet #10
Values Clarification

Compare your life to Kino's. Under the "Necessities" columns, list the things that you value most. Then list the things Kino values most. Do the same thing under the "Luxuries" columns, listing the things you consider luxuries and the things Kino would consider luxuries.

Kino's Necessities	My Necessities

Kino's Luxuries	My Luxuries

Name_____

The Pearl
Final Exam

I. Multiple Choice. Indicate the answer that best completes each statement.

1. Kino lives
   a. in a city
   b. next door to the doctor
   c. near the beach
   d. in the jungle

2. In the morning, Kino seems to hear the waves on the beach singing the "Song of the Family." The meaning is that Kino
   a. dislikes having to earn his living in a boat
   b. is not fully sane
   c. feels that it is good for his family to earn their living by working closely with nature
   d. knows that his people had once been great makers of song

3. We are told in the first chapter that Kino's people "had once been great makers of songs so that everything they saw or thought or did or heard became a song." It is important to note this statement because
   a. it gives one an insight into the abnormal mental wanderings of a suppressed and deprived people
   b. depending on what kind of music Kino seems to sense, he gets an intuitive feeling as to whether a person or situation is good or evil
   c. music can be an important feature in controlling poisonous insects or reptiles
   d. the emphasis in this story is on man's lack of dignity and similarity to animals

4. When Kino is said to hear music, the reader is supposed to see that life has its own subtle patterns and rhythms whereby
   a. Kino judges a situation intuitively
   b. the author is showing by contrast his own cultural background
   c. Kino is showing himself as quite an elderly man, yet capable of strong action
   d. man should, in trying to decide on a course of action, shun primitive urges and instincts since such things are basically corrupt

5. The main characters in this story
   a. usually are quite talkative
   b. usually wear protective boots
   c. understand that they are part of an underprivileged race
   d. show no tolerance for wealthy people

Name_____

The Pearl
Final Exam • 2

6. Right after the baby is stung by the scorpion, Juana puts her lips down over the puncture and sucks and spits while Coyotito screams. She does this
   a. as part of an ancient magic ritual to guard against evil
   b. to draw out the poison before it can get into the bloodstream
   c. from a peculiar morbid curiosity
   d. because she wants to die with her child

7. The neighbors think it a "wonderful thing, a memorable thing" to want the doctor because
   a. Juana had not believed in doctors before
   b. her people usually went to medicine men or used folk remedies
   c. the lazy doctor cared only for the rich and didn't tend poor Indians
   d. Coyotito was Juana's first baby

8. The town's best expert(s) in financial analysis
   a. were the beggars
   b. was the doctor
   c. used to force Juan Tomás to meet unjust interest payments
   d. went to the doctor regularly

9. When the doctor says, "I am a doctor, not a veterinary," he shows
   a. anger at having been called to treat an insect bite
   b. just anger at the town's ignorance
   c. great sympathy for those who are sick and downtrodden
   d. that he thinks of the natives as animals

10. When Juana takes the pearl to the church, Kino thinks
    a. that she is going to give it to the priest
    b. that she is praying for a miracle
    c. that the time has come for him to think more deeply about life
    d. no such incident occurs; Juana does not take the pearl to the church

11. The doctor knows where Kino's pearl is buried because
    a. Kino's brother unconsciously gave away the secret
    b. the doctor knows the ways of the peasants
    c. the doctor's servant had seen a few specks of dirt loose on the cottage floor
    d. the doctor had seen Kino's eyes go to the hiding place

Name_____

The Pearl
Final Exam • 3

12. As Kino and the procession following him approached, the pearl buyers put away all the pearls on their desks because
    a. they were afraid that some would get lost or stolen
    b. it is not good to let an inferior pearl be seen beside a beauty
    c. Kino might decide not to sell his pearl if he saw the others
    d. the employer of the pearl buyers might hear that they were hoarding pearls

13. At one time the people had hired agents to sell their pearls in the city, but they were never heard from again. The people took this
    a. with angry resentment
    b. as divine punishment
    c. as another example of the doctor's greedy background operations
    d. with cheerful confidence that they could always find more pearls

14. When the buyer sees the size and beauty of Kino's pearl, he shows his surprise
    a. by dropping the coin he had been skillfully handling
    b. with a sudden burst of profanity
    c. in a slight change of expression
    d. by raising the price he had planned to offer

15. After his house burns, Kino is able to get supplies
    a. from his brother   c. by stealing
    b. from his sister   d. on credit

16. The first time Kino kills someone, the weapon is a
    a. rifle   b. shotgun   c. harpoon   d. knife

17. Which of the following is NOT one of the things Kino does to hide footprints as he and his wife leave home?
    a. walk in the wheel rut
    b. walk where the blowing sand will cover the tracks
    c. walk backward
    d. sweep the footprints with a branch

18. Which of the following statements is NOT true about the pearl?
    a. It was the biggest pearl ever seen by most of the people.
    b. It was so big the pearl buyers knew it was not worth much.
    c. It made Kino abandon the things which are truly important and attempt to buy dignity.
    d. It might be the only chance Kino and his family would have to raise their status.

Name_____

The Pearl
Final Exam • 4

19. How many people chase Kino and Juana out of town?
    a. one   b. two   c. three   d. four

20. Kino figures that in order to attack his trackers successfully he must
    a. take off his clothes
    b. wait for the moon to come out
    c. lure them to the cave
    d. rub dirt on his knife

21. When the trackers hear a murmuring cry in the distance at night, they suppose it to be
    a. Coyotito   b. an owl   c. a coyote   d. an omen

22. Coyotito is
    a. killed instantly by a tracker firing his rifle toward the cave
    b. murdered in cold blood by Kino's pursuers
    c. accidentally suffocated by Juana when she tried to keep him quiet
    d. able at last to go to school

23. When the author says that Kino saw evil faces and frantic eyes in the pearl, he is telling the reader in a dramatic way that
    a. the experiences of the chase have driven Kino insane
    b. Kino now sees the evil of having the pearl
    c. the story has actually been a dream
    d. Kino is now dead

24. At the end of the story, Kino
    a. sold the pearl
    b. threw the pearl into the sea
    c. gave the pearl to his brother
    d. swallowed the pearl and died

25. This story shows that, no matter how exalted or how lowly their possessions, surroundings, or means to a living, humans
    a. must never try to change their lot in life
    b. must always revisit the scenes of their crimes
    c. cannot rise in status if they are members of an oppressed race
    d. get their dignity and happiness from a realization of who they *are*, not what they *have*

26. Juana had prayed directly for
    a. the baby's recovery
    b. the help of the doctor
    c. a large pearl
    d. the will of God to be done

27. As he searched for oysters, Kino sang
    a. the Song of the Family
    b. the Song of the Undersea
    c. the Song of Evil
    d. the Song of the Oyster

Name_____

The Pearl
Final Exam • 5

28. After discovering the pearl, the first thing Kino said he wanted to do was
    a. marry Juana in the church
    b. build a stone and plaster house
    c. buy another canoe
    d. call the doctor for the baby

29. Pulque is a drink made from
    a. fermented rice   b. cactus juice   c. agave juice   d. kiwi fruit

30. To pretend he could cure the baby, the doctor gave him
    a. quinine   b. aspirin   c. sugar capsules   d. ammonia

True-False: Choose A if the statement is true; choose B if it is false.

____31. Kino is at least able to catch the scorpion and kill it.
____32. Kino never liked the doctor because he was of another race.
____33. Although the doctor is really at home when the family goes there, he tells his servant to say he is out on a serious call.
____34. Kino was proud of the boat he had built.
____35. Since Kino and Juana had been married in the village church, the priest knew they would be happy to help with the necessary repairs.
____36. There is really only one pearl buyer. The other men act as his agents and give the appearance that they are competing.
____37. Kino and Juana resented the neighbors' insistence on accompanying them to the town to sell the pearl.
____38. Kino has made his living primarily from fishing, although at times he also searched for pearls.
____39. When Kino says, "I am a man," Juana knows this means he will try to drive his strength against anything.
____40. Kino was not a man to be content with what he had. He felt compelled to strive for more.

Vocabulary: Choose the best definition for each word.

41. **estuary:**   a. encampment   b. plain   c. river mouth

42. **lethargy:**   a. drowsiness   b. defense   c. lesson

43. **poultice:**   a. venom   b. kelp   c. dressing

44. **germane:**   a. closely related   b. worried   c. avarice

45. **speculative:** a. obscure   b. skillful   c. thoughtful

Name_____

The Pearl
Final Exam • 6

46.	**petulant:**	a. malignant	b. flowery	c. impatient
47.	**suppliant:**	a. athletic	b. worried	c. humble
48.	**monolithic:**	a. monotonous	b. monumental	c. momentous
49.	**bulwark:**	a. greed	b. defense	c. giant
50.	**indigent:**	a. intelligent	b. insane	c. poor
51.	**feinted:**	a. pretended	b. swooned	c. passed out
52.	**hummock:**	a. hill	b. hammock	c. humble
53.	**judicious:**	a. wise	b. humorous	c. benign
54.	**furtive:**	a. ditch	b. brave	c. sneaky
55.	**stalwart:**	a. late	b. strong	c. dishonest

Cause and Effect: Link the causes in the first column with the effects in the second column by indicating the correct letter.

56. Coyotito is everything to Juana___
57. The doctor's race has persecuted Kino's race for centuries___
58. Kino is afraid to want something too much___
59. Other people are envious of Kino's good fortune___
60. The doctor hears that Kino found the pearl___
61. The pearl buyers cheat Kino___
62. Juana tries to throw the pearl away___
63. Kino is ambushed coming back from the beach___
64. Kino's canoe is ruined___
65. Coyotito cries out___

A. so Kino decides to go to the capital
B. so he is angry and yet ashamed
C. so they try to steal the pearl
D. so the family must walk to the capital
E. so Kino follows and beats her
F. so he is mistaken for an animal and killed
G. so she wants to see the doctor
H. so he kills a man with his knife
I. so he waits to open the big oyster
J. so he comes to see the baby

Essay: Write a well-developed answer for each question. Be sure to include supporting details and an effective conclusion.

1. Discuss the significance of the various songs which go through Kino's mind. What purposes do these songs serve in the novel?

2. Analyze the character of either Juana or Kino, or analyze the progression of their relationship as the novel unfolds.

Answer Key

Student Worksheets
#1:
1. a fermented drink made of the juice of the agave, or American aloe
2. a climbing, flowering tropical plant
3. books about horticulture or botany
4. pertaining to lymph nodes
5. a spider-like insect with a long tail and a stinger
6. a book about biology
7. a book about insects
8. A supple limb is flexible and easily bent; a suppliant person bends to the will of others.
9. A substitute is second to the original; something that is subsequent comes after.
10. A coven is a group of witches; a covey is a group of partridges or quail.
11. B
12. A
13. D
14. C

#2
1. crest
2. defray
3. bullock
4. hammock
5. stimulant
6. validated
7. oasis
8. subdued
9. I
10. B
11. F
12. H
13. L
14. D
15. J
16. A
17. K
18. C
19. G
20. E

#3
Students' answers will vary, but should include several synonyms and antonyms (if the word has antonyms), the word's origin, a definition, and the word used in a sentence.

#4
(Examples only)
sinister-evil-malevolent-ominous; **guttural**-hoarse-gruff-throaty; **monolithic**-monumental-massive-imposing; **irresolution**-indecision-vacillation-fluctuation; **escarpment**-cliff-precipice-promontory; **petulant**-fretful-irritable-cross; **intercession**-arbitration-intervention-mediation; **germane**-relevant-pertinent-apropos

Study Guide
1. Kino, Juana, Coyotito
2. (See p. 4.) Kino was young and strong with black hair hung over his brown forehead. His eyes were warm and fierce and bright, and his mustache was thin and coarse.
   (See p. 5.) Juana had black hair that she combed and braided in two braids tied with ribbon. Her dark eyes made little reflected stars (p. 2). (See p. 9.) She was patient and fragile, obedient, respectful, and cheerful. Coyotito, the baby, is usually described as laughing.
3. They are extremely poor, living in a brush house and eating very simply. They fish for a living and are not educated.
4. (See p. 7.) They believe in the songs of their ancestors. Juana "whispers little magics" over the baby.
5. Ants (See pp. 3-4.)
   Personification of fire (See p. 3.)
   Kino and Juana (See pp. 4-5, 9.)
   Doctor (See p. 11.)
   How a pearl is made (See p. 21.)
6. Finding the pearl
7. Kino's people had once been great makers of song (see p. 2). The feeling he has when he arises is represented by the Song of the Family—"the whole." When the scorpion stings the baby, Kino hears the Song of Evil. After the baby is bitten, the Song of the Enemy prevails. By including the songs, Steinbeck enables the reader to understand Kino's emotions and also adds to his portrayal as a person close to the native traditions.
8. See pp. 10-11 for the physical differences. We are made genuinely aware of the differences when the doctor refuses to treat Coyotito.
9. a. See p. 11 for the beggars' description.
   b. See pp. 13-14 for the doctor's own feelings.
   c. See p. 12 for Kino's analysis of the doctor.
10. See p. 17 for a description of the canoes.
    See p. 18 for a description of hungry animals looking for food.
    See pp. 18-19 for a description of illusion vs. reality.
    These descriptions should help the students make an obvious inference about the villagers in each of these situations.

© Novel Units, Inc.   All rights reserved

11. The canoe was passed down from generation to generation and was not just property but also a source of income. (See p. 19.)
12. See p. 21 for a description of how pearls are made.
13. See pp. 22-23.
14. They sing songs to give them strength in bad situations and to bring exhilaration in good times, i.e., the Song of the Undersea when Kino is looking for pearls.
15. He thinks it contains a large pearl, but is afraid it is bad luck to want something too much.
16. The swelling in Coyotito's shoulder subsides. Juana sees it as a miracle.
17. They were envious; had their own ideas of how Kino's pearl could help them.
18. the scorpion; hunger; loneliness
19. If Coyotito learns to read, Juana and Kino will not be so victimized by the Spaniards.
20. He told them the baby needed medicine, but what he gave him made the baby sicker.
21. When someone came to steal the pearl, Kino chased them away but was hit on the head.
22. a. Kino has never sold a pearl before. He doesn't know its real value.
    b. Kino knows his ancestors have been cheated in the past. His instinct tells him this is a very valuable pearl.
23. The dealers already knew Kino would bring the pearl, and had planned what to say and how much to offer.
24. The townspeople's reactions vary from admiration of Kino to the conviction that he is foolish.
25. Kino has decided to go to the capital to sell his pearl. He believes that the pearl buyers are trying to cheat him; this is his motivation to go to the capital.
26. Juana takes the pearl while she thinks Kino is asleep. She wants to get rid of it.
27. Kino assaulted Juana for taking the pearl.
28. Kino stabbed and killed a man; their house was burned; the canoe was destroyed.
29. Hiding in Juan Tomás' house while Juan gathered supplies for their trip.
30. The pearl has become his soul. He is determined to reap the material benefits that he knows should be his.
31. (See p. 90.) He is described as having an animal inside him.
32. Kino and his family flee the village./ They hide in a covert when trackers approach./ They begin a frantic flight to the high country./ They decide to hide in a cave./ Kino throws the trackers off by backtracking./ Kino plans a way to kill all three trackers./ Before he can complete his plan, one of the trackers fires a rifle, and the bullet kills Coyotito./ Kino kills all three men.
33. Ironically, one of Kino's wishes has come true: he has a rifle. Juana carries the baby's body. They are like two dead spirits. (See pp. 115-116.)
34. and 35. Answers will vary.

Vocabulary Quiz
1. C
2. F
3. H
4. G
5. I
6. L
7. M
8. E
9. D
10. N
11. A
12. B
13. J
14. O
15. K

Chapter One Quiz
1. dark haired, brown-skinned, young, strong
2. It represents the feelings Kino has for his family.
3. a scorpion
4. She whispers an old magic chant when Kino is trying to get the scorpion away from the baby.
5. the four beggars
6. His race has subjugated Kino's for centuries.
7. Juana and Kino have no money.
8. poor native
9. France
10. out on a serious case

Chapters Two & Three Quiz
1. a river mouth or inlet
2. his grandfather made it; it means food and money
3. a large pearl to pay the doctor
4. The pearl is an accident of nature, and Kino's chances of finding it were slim.
5. The swelling subsided.
6. Any of these: a proper marriage; new clothes; a rifle; a harpoon; education for Coyotito
7. He tells them the poison may still be in the baby's system. He causes the baby to be temporarily ill with the powder, then pretends to heal him with the ammonia.
8. Student answers will vary but should be supported with explanations.
9. He becomes determined and vengeful.
10. She feels it is evil.

Chapter Four Quiz

1. La Paz
2. Everyone in the village went along.
3. They appeared to be competing, but really all worked for one agent.
4. No. Their main objective was to cheat them.
5. They pretended the pearl was of poor quality and that they really weren't very interested in buying it.
6. He decided to sell it in the capital.
7. They admired him for taking a stand against the injustice they all lived with.
8. Juan Tomás felt Kino should not try to overstep his societal boundaries.
9. his friends
10. She wants to destroy the pearl.

Chapter Five Quiz

1. She wants to throw the pearl into the sea.
2. He brutally assaults her.
3. She knows she could not survive without him.
4. He was ambushed, and killed the attacker.
5. It rolled away behind a stone.
6. because he has killed a man
7. A hole was broken in it.
8. It was burned.
9. He hid them at his house, got supplies for them.
10. give it up

Chapter Six Quiz

1. an animal, a hunter, a killer
2. walks in wheel ruts, covers tracks, backtracks
3. two on foot, one on horseback with a rifle
4. to keep her and the baby out of danger
5. in a cave
6. He plans to attack the one on watch, get his rifle, and kill the other two.
7. Coyotito was killed by a bullet from the rifle fired in the direction of the cave.
8. They walk like dead spirits, side by side, carrying the rifle and the dead baby.
9. Kino threw it into the sea.
10. They have each other, their friends (whom they no longer trust), their relatives (whom they do), and, ironically, a rifle.

Final Exam

1. C
2. C
3. B
4. A
5. C
6. B
7. C
8. A
9. D
10. D
11. D
12. B
13. B
14. A
15. A
16. D
17. C
18. B
19. C
20. A
21. C
22. A
23. B
24. B
25. D
26. C
27. B
28. A
29. C
30. D
31. A
32. B
33. A
34. B
35. B
36. A
37. B
38. A
39. A
40. A
41. C
42. A
43. C
44. A
45. C
46. C
47. C
48. B
49. B
50. C
51. A
52. A
53. A
54. C
55. B
56. G
57. B
58. I
59. C
60. J
61. A
62. E
63. H
64. D
65. F

Essay: Students' answers will vary somewhat, but should include some of the points outlined below.

1. The Song of the Family represents the love and contentment Kino feels when he looks at or hears Juana and Coyotito. It is tied to the way he makes his living—from nature—and to a feeling of warmth and security. The family is the Whole. Kino hears the Song of Evil throughout the book. It begins when the scorpion stings the baby, and is later associated with the doctor, the priest, the pearl buyers, and those who try to steal the pearl. The Song of the Enemy often plays along with the Song of Evil and is associated with the same things. The Song of the Undersea celebrates the sea and all its creatures, and plays over the Song of the Pearl That Might Be. Steinbeck included the songs to let the reader know that Kino is still deeply connected to his native roots. Intuition substitutes for the education he does not have. They let us know how Kino is feeling.

2. Juana is fragile-looking, patient, loyal, and obedient for the most part, but she also has a mind of her own. She insists on taking the baby to the doctor, and later on tries to get rid of the pearl herself. She seems to show more strength and sensibility as the novel progresses. Kino is brave for attempting to break out of the rut of poverty and ignorance. He seems to be butting his head against a wall, for there is nothing but evil against him. His attempts to buy dignity fail. The couple's relationship changes in that they become more equal for having shared so much pain.

Notes